IN TIMES

Wood Green and Tottenham
with
West Green and Harringay

An Illustrated Journey
into
More Peaceful Life Styles

by
PETER CURTIS

HORNSEY HISTORICAL SOCIETY

PUBLISHED IN 1991
2nd Edition 1992
(with minor amendments)
3rd Edition 1995
(with further amendments)

by The Hornsey Historical Society,
The Old Schoolhouse,
136 Tottenham Lane,
LONDON N8 7EL

ISBN 0 095794 07 9

Cover Design by Richard Robertson

Set in 11 point Times Roman, by Pennant Press

Printed and bound in Great Britain by
J.G. Bryson (Printer) Ltd.,
156-162 High Road, East Finchley, London N2 9AS

CONTENTS

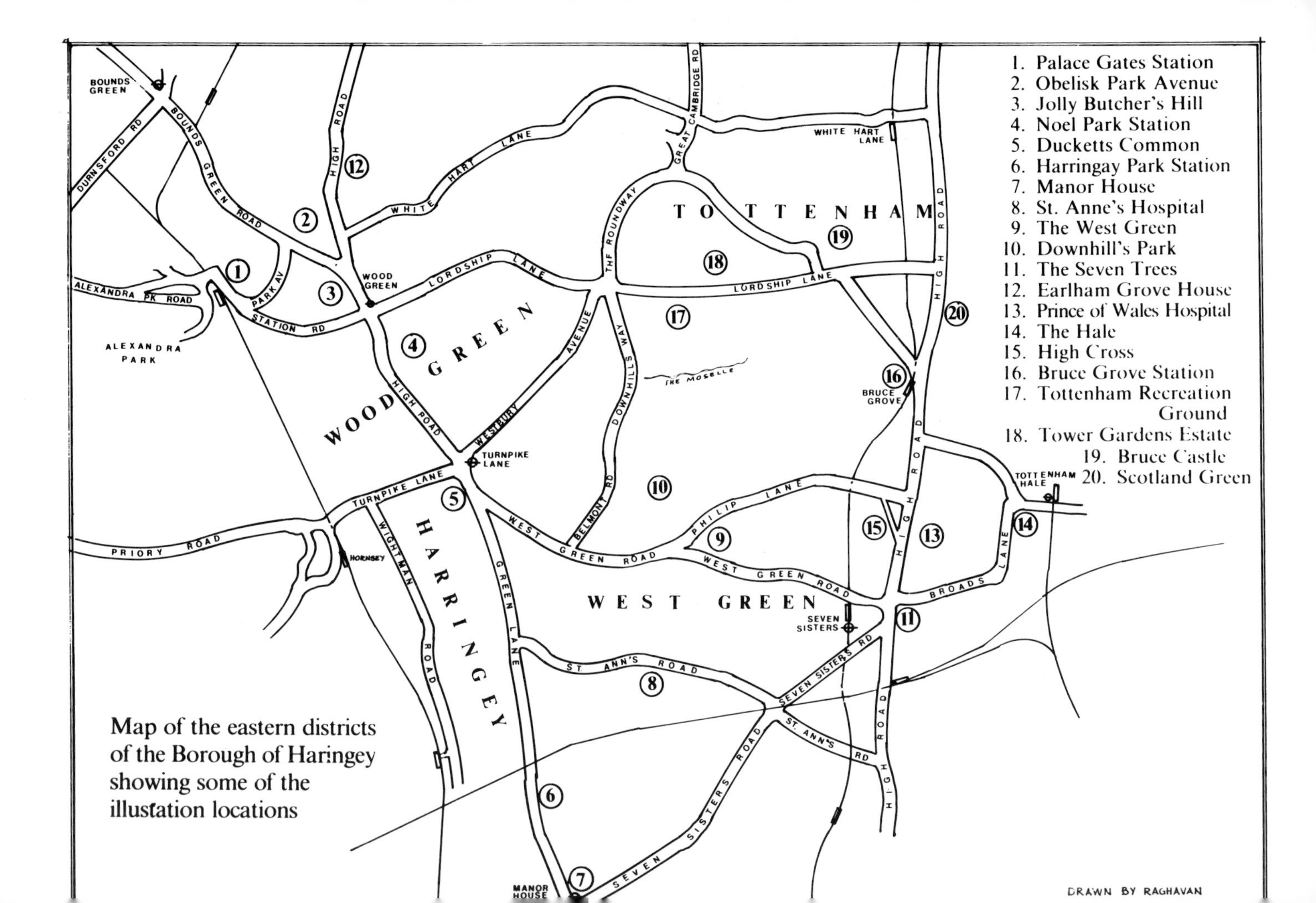

Map of the eastern districts of the Borough of Haringey showing some of the illustation locations

"In Times Past"

PREFACE

This book includes over a hundred photographs covering the central and eastern districts of the London Borough of Harringey, illustrating the most dramatic part of a period of change that has stretched from 1850 to the present day.

Many readers will remember buildings that have been swept away. They will see how fashions have changed — what the well dressed couple wore in 1910, for instance. The pictures show how people got to work in late Victorian and Edwardian times, when transport was radically different from today. We can see how family shopping was catered for before the first World War. How the area materialised is gradually unfolded, remembering that farmland existed until the 1930s. We can begin to see when the local population increased and why.

66 photographs are from Bruce Castle Museum's archives, 23 from Dick Whetstone's postcard collection, and 12 from the Hornsey Historical Society's archives. All are reproduced here with detailed notes on each view and introductions to the history of each district.

The illustrations could not have been assembled nor the text written without a team effort. I am indebted to Ken Gay, Susan Hector, Rag Raghavan and Malcolm Stokes for their research and contributions. And to Joan Schwitzer for her invaluable advice. We are all members of Hornsey Historical Society.

Thanks also to our long suffering type setters and printers for their patience.

Much help was given by the Curator and staff, in particular Rita Read, of Bruce Castle museum. Here I should like to draw attention to the facilities for research into the history of all parts of Harringay at the museum (Lordship Lane, Tottenham, London N17 8NU. Telephone 020-8808 8772), We are especially grateful to Dick Whetstone for access to his unique historical collection.

WOOD GREEN

Wood Green as we know it today was largely built up in the last quarter of the 19th century. In the 1840s Wood Green was little more than a scattered settlement on Green Lanes, around its junction with Lordship Lane, set in pleasant countryside a few miles north of London. Its villas and cottages housed less than 500 people. *The Three Jolly Butchers* and *The Nags Head* in earlier rural form were the local hostelries, catering for livestock-drovers and others coming into London.

In 1844 a chapel-of-ease called St. Michael's was built north of Jolly Butchers Hill to cater for an increasing population. Wood Green was part of the ancient parish of Tottenham and the new chapel saved Wood Green residents the journey to the parish church of All Hallows, which still stands near to Bruce Castle.

The countryside was used as a place for leisure and retirement by Londoners. Almshouses were built in the area by different charities and the Freemasons opened a boys' school in Lordship Lane in 1857. Farmlands to the west were acquired in 1863 on which Alexandra Park was laid out and the first Alexandra Palace built, opened in 1873. The Ordnance Survey map of the area published in 1873 shows no buildings between Lorship Lane and present day Turnpike Lane along the line of the present day High Road, except for Dovecote House (Ducketts) and Dovecote Villas. Green Lanes, as it was then called was lined with fields.

By contrast the 1894 Ordnance Survey map shows the same area covered with streets of terraced houses each side of the High Road. Change had followed the coming of the railways. In 1859 Wood Green railway station had been opened on the west, on the Great Northern line out of Kings Cross. The first residential development had been in the 1860s in the triangle of land north of St Michael's church, mainly semi-detached villas for the middle classes. Caxton and Mayes roads were also laid out further south, west of Green Lanes. These roads can all be seen on the 1873 OS map. Major developments to the south of Lordship Lane followed by the opening of the 1878 railway line from east London through Seven Sisters to Palace Gates station. This line crossed Green Lanes about one quarter of a mile north of Turnpike Lane. A station was opened here called 'Green Lanes', later 'Noel Park and Wood Green'.

From 1883 onwards, east of the High Road, the extensive Noel Park estate began to be built up on 100 acres of the former Ducketts farmlands. Devised by the Artizans', Labourers' and General Dwellings Company to provide good housing, it accommodated 7,000 people by 1886, with building continuing, but mostly completed by 1907. Along the High Road by it the Cheapside shopping parade and Wood Green Empire had been built by 1912. By this time the High Road was lined with Victorian age shopping parades and in the 20th century Wood Green was to become a notable shopping centre.

By the late 1880s Wood Green had grown sufficiently for its inhabitants to demand their own local government, separate from Tottenham. Tottenham was also being built up intensively at this time, but was still separated from Wood Green by farmlands. In 1888 Wood Green gained its own local Board and in 1894 it became an Urban District Council. In 1933 it was to become a Borough. By 1890 Earlham Grove House, standing in its own park, east of Green Lanes to the north of Wood Green, had become the headquarters of local government. Purchased with 11 acres in 1893 it was to remain the headquarters until 1958 when the new Wood Green Civic centre (now Haringey Civic Centre) was opened a little further south on the other side of Wood Green High Road, near St Michael's church, on the site of demolished almshouses.

Well served by public transport, Wood Green developed as a middle class residential suburb, with many local people travelling into London to work, many of them clerks, using the railways or buses, trams and trolleybuses. Local employment was provided by a few factories, mostly located near the main line GNR railway, of which the most notable was probably Barratts the confectioners, in Mayes Road from 1880. The extension of the Piccadilly tube line through the area in 1932, with stations at Turnpike Lane, Wood Green and Bounds Green encouraged more building and further commuter traffic into London, and strengthened Wood Green as an important shopping centre. These inter-war developments included a large cinema and adjacent shopping parades built beside the High Road, across from the Noel Park estate in 1934, buildings which still stand; and another large cinema near Turnpike Lane tube station opened as the Ritz in 1935, and demolished in 1999.

Wood Green remained essentially late-Victorian or Edwardian in structure till after the Second World War. In the 1950s and 1960s the two sets of almhouse buildings near St Michael's church disappeared for new buildings and *The Three Jolly Butchers* became part of a new office block. In the 1970s, the 1907 Carnegie civic library opposite the Wood Green tube station was replaced by a tall, office building, and new office blocks began to line Station Road. More significantly the now disused Noel Park station and railway line site was used to build the modern Wood Green shopping city. North of it was built the new Haringey central library and beyond it, in the 1980s, a new supermarket. Haringey Council, formed in 1965 from the Boroughs of Wood Green, Tottenham and Hornsey, had other plans for leisure buildings and road changes in this area but these were not carried through.

The pictures in this volume show a Victorian and Edwardian Wood Green which is recognisable and largely still in existence. Its importance as a shopping centre has increased and it is a convenient place for working Londoners to live, with 200 acres of Alexandra Park, in public ownership since 1901, to be enjoyed.

Ken Gay

A public house called The Three Jolly Butchers has stood west of Green Lanes on the hill by the junction with Bounds Green Road at least since the eighteenth century, and the hill was named after it. The original inn would have served travellers bringing livestock and produce along Green Lanes to the London market and the inn might have been named after butcher customers. Till the last half of the nineteenth century the way south through Wood Green would have been through fields with very little settlement. After Wood Green was developed as a suburb the inn was rebuilt and was to be rebuilt again in the 1960s.

(Picture Bruce Castle).

The Three Jolly Butchers, Wood Green, 1890

The Three Jolly Butchers, Wood Green, 1910

The public house which replaced the old inn at the turn of the nineteenth century was in fairly florid style with corner cupola and large outside lamps. It was demolished and replaced with an office block incorporating a new public house with the same name in the 1960s.

(Picture, Bruce Castle).

Looking towards St Michael's church. The metal post on the left supports the electricity supply cables for the tramcars, once a distinctive feature of the road scene. Goods delivery is by horse and cart; the one on the left is from Edmonds Brothers, then one of the larger stores in Wood Green High Road. Some of the shops on the right at the corner of Lordship Lane were demolished in 1931 to make way for Wood Green tube station.

(Picture, Bruce Castle).

Jolly Butchers Hill, Wood Green, c.1910

Jolly Butchers Hill, Wood Green, c.1910

Another view up the hill towards St Michael's church. Postmen wearing 'shako' helmets stand on the left. The tramcar on the far right is one of the original Metropolitan Electric Tramways Company type A vehicles on its way to Finsbury Park. The type H tramcar on the left of it is bound for Palmers Green.

(Picture, Dick Whetstone).

This view is down the hill towards the Lordship Lane junction and seems to have been taken from the entrance to the transport depot. Horse trams began to run between Manor House and Wood Green in 1887. When electric trams were introduced in 1904 the company established its depot on Jolly Butchers Hill on a site previously used for the horse trams. Subsequently the depot housed trolley buses and today diesel buses.

(Picture, Dick Whetstone).

Jolly Butchers Hill, Wood Green, c.1910

Horse transport, Wood Green, 1891

This late-Victorian photograph, taken at the junction of Lordship Lane and the High Road, shows horse buses, horse trams and bicycles as the means of transport. Horse buses had started running between Wood Green and the City by 1856. Horse trams began to operate from Finsbury Park via Manor House to Wood Green in 1887.

(Picture, HHS).

The view of the corner of Jolly Butchers Hill and Lordship Lane was taken in 1930 shortly before demolition. Wood Green tube station opened on this site on 19th September 1932 when the Piccadilly line was extended north from Finsbury Park, eventually to Cockfosters. Shops up the hill to the left, and round the corner in Lordship Lane to the right, still remain today. Traffic lights now control the junction.

(Picture, Bruce Castle).

Site of Wood Green tube station, c.1930

St Michael's Church, Wood Green, 1903

Situated at the junction of High Road and Bounds Green Road. Sir George Gilbert Scott and W.B.Moffat were the original architects of this Church of England building, erected as a chapel in 1844 but enlarged to cater for a growing population in 1863. On the west side (left) can be seen part of the Printers' Almshouses, designed by William Webb. Opened for 12 couples in 1856 they were enlarged in 1871 and 1891. The almshouses were demolished and a telecommunications centre opened on their site in 1974.

(Picture, Bruce Castle).

These gardens are situated opposite St Michael's church, between Wood Green High Road (left) and Stuart Crescent. They occupy former roadside common land. The War Memorial was placed at the southern end, and the area was subsequently renamed King George VI Memorial Gardens. The Kings Arms public house (centre) is just south of Kings Road. Like the Fishmongers' Arms on the opposite side of the High Road from it (left) it has Assembly Rooms attached to it, used for entertainments of various kinds. The Fishmongers' Arms took its name from the 1850 Fishmongers' and Poulterers' Almshouses, once situated in the High Road opposite Crescent Gardens, but demolished to make way for the 1958 Wood Green Civic Centre now occupying the site.

(Picture, Bruce Castle).

16207 CRESCENT GARDENS. WOOD GREEN.

Crescent Gardens, Wood Green, 1910

Wood Green Town Hall, c.1910

Earlham Grove House was built on the east side of Wood Green High Road opposite Nightingale Road, in about 1865. Here once lived Mrs Catherine Smithies *(see page 23)*. By 1890 it was occupied by Wood Green Local Board (created in 1888 when local residents gained their own administration separate from Tottenham) and purchased by the Board, along with about 11 acres of land, in 1893. The mansion was used as the Town Hall until 1958. Now named Woodside House the building is used as a social centre by elderly people and others, and the grounds for recreation. An early garden building (listed), possibly built as an ornamental dairy, survives in the north west corner. The house and grounds are a solitary local reminder of the big estates which the wealthy built in this once rural part of Middlesex.

(Picture, HHS)

This view of Earlham Grove House (now Woodside House) shows the extension (right) built in 1913 to accommodate a new council chamber and a court room. Wood Green Local Board of Health, created in 1888, was superseded by Wood Green Urban District Council in 1894 and in 1933 Wood Green became a borough. This building continued as the town hall until 1958 when a new civic centre was opened on the opposite side of Wood Green High Road, further south. In 1965, the borough of Wood Green was joined to the boroughs of Tottenham and Hornsey to form the new London Borough of Haringey, and Haringey Council meets in the council chamber in the former Wood Green civic centre.

(Picture, Bruce Castle).

Wood Green, Town Hall, 1913

Commerce Road, Wood Green, 1910

The earliest development of Wood Green occurred in the angle of land between Bounds Green Lane (later Road) and Green Lanes (later Wood Green High Road). In the 1860s Commerce, Nightingale, Finsbury, Truro and Clarence Roads were laid out and built up, as first with detached and semi-detached villas. Much of the High Road end of Commerce Road was developed with shops to serve the local community and here we are looking west.

(Picture, HHS)

Another view showing the block of shops to the right of those in the previous picture. The shops were built from the High Road as far as Finsbury Road, which runs across Commerce Road, parallel to the New River (see page 17).

(Picture, HHS).

Commerce Road, Wood Green, c.1910

Myddleton Road, Wood Green, c.1903

Laid out between Green Lanes and Bowes Park railway station, near the northern boundary of Wood Green in Bowes Park, a district named after a former local estate. The district developed significantly after 1880 when Bowes Park railway station was opened on the 1871 branch line from Wood Green to Enfield. The road became popular for shopping but has declined in recent years because of changing shopping habits. Myddleton Road is named after Sir Hugh Myddleton who built the early 17th century water course called the New River, bringing drinking water into London. The river used to loop towards the east of Wood Green and curve back along the line of River Park Road (near Station Road). In 1852 the river course was shortened and water channelled through this area, across Bounds Green Road and under Avenue Gardens. In Myddleton Road is a listed mid-19th century tunnel entrance to the New River.

(Picture, HHS)

Newnham Road, looking west to the junction with Canning Crescent (centre) which runs into Wood Green High Road opposite Commerce Road. The children are facing towards Riversdale Gardens, the name another reminder of the former course of the New River. East of these gardens are White Hart Lane Recreation Grounds containing schools, variously named during this century. The Unitarians built a church and hall in Newnham Road (left, off picture) in 1902, since demolished.

(Picture, Dick Whetstone)

Newnham Road, Wood Green, c. 1910

White Hart Lane, Wood Green, 1912

The Lane remained rural until the early 1930's. Tottenham Potteries, Devonshire Hill Farm and Rectory Farm on the east side were working in the early 1920s. Tottenham Grammar School (latterly Somerset School) was built in the 1930s near the Tottenham end; it was demolished in 1989 to make way for housing. Much of the western end from White Hart Lane School to Fenton Road remains pleasantly open with Playing fields and the well equipped New River Sports and Recreation Centre.

(Picture, Bruce Castle).

The infants School built c.1900 had a large assembly hall on the ground floor and class rooms seating 40-50 young pupils at tiered desks. This way they could see the teacher and blackboard or more importantly the teacher could see them and deal with any inattentive child. Later the school served for many years as an Adult Education centre to be closed in 1990 and demolished for housing.

(Picture, Bruce Castle)

White Hart Lane School, Wood Green, 1906

White Hart Lane School, Wood Green, 1906

The neatly dressed infants sit at tiered desks for a drawing lesson, presumably of a pair of cherries

(Picture, Bruce Castle).

This rural lane leads from White Hart Lane past St Cuthbert's Church, which had been built in 1907 to designs by architect J.S. Alder. The fields on each side were farmed by Devonshire Hill Farm. The milkman left of picture is on his milk rounds. Perhaps the other people are on their way to morning service. Today the New River Sports and Recreation Centre occupy the fields on the east side while on the west housing was built along roads leading to Green Lanes.

(Picture, Bruce Castle).

Wolves Lane, Wood Green, 1910

Bounds Green Road, Wood Green, c.1900

Looking south towards St. Michael's church. Some early nineteenth century listed houses survive opposite the church. In the middle distance is the secondary school opened in 1899 which became variously known as Trinity County, Parkwood and St Thomas More. The obelisk monument is to Mrs Catherine Smithies. Formerly resident in Earlham Grove house (*see page 13*), Mrs Smithies was devoted to charitable works and founded the Band of Mercy Movement, and organisation whose object was to teach children the moral and Christian duties of kindness to animals. The memorial was presented by her family and friends with a public drinking fountain at its base (but unfortunately it no longer operates). When erected in 1879 it stood at the road junction with Park Avenue (right) as illustrated. Subsequently it was moved out of the way of traffic into Finsbury Gardens (left) where it now stands.

(Picture, C. R. Smith Publications).

Station Road leads past still surviving Wood Green common and past Avenue Gardens to Wood Green railway station, opened in 1859 on the Great Northern line out of Kings Cross. The station was renamed Alexandra Palace in 1982. The hotel building stands opposite the station on the corner of St Michael's Terrace; beyond it are the houses of Buckingham Road, the continuation of Station Road. The hotel is dated 1875, the year the second Alexandra Palace was opened. It was subsequently known as the Alexandra Palace and Railway Hotel and then the Railway Hotel. In the 1960s it was renamed The Starting Gate, in reference to the racecourse which existed in nearby Alexandra Park from 1868 until September 1970. The General Post Office established the Wood Green N22 District Sorting Office near the railway station in Terrick Road behind the hotel. Later the GPO extended their premises onto the site next to the hotel in Buckingham Road; the building is dated 1952.

(Picture, Bruce Castle).

The Alexandra Palace Hotel, Wood Green, c.1902

Crescent Road, Alexandra Park, Wood Green, c.1910

The view is from the road bridge across the railway, just north of Wood Green station (now Alexandra Palace), looking towards the junction with Palace Gates Road (middle distance, left). Development of the area of Wood Green west of the Great Northern railway and north of Alexandra Park did not occur much before the end of the nineteenth century. The building on the extreme right (which is next to the road bridge) probably dates from the 1880s, but the terrace of shops next to it, where the horse and cart stands, is dated 1898. Today the junction triangle (centre) is a paved area where a polling booth is put up at election times. The building on the extreme left has gone and a post war building is on the site. Otherwise the view is unchanged, except for parked vehicles and almost constant traffic.

(Picture, Dick Whetstone)

This view is taken in the stretch of the road which leads from the station and looks westwards up the hill towards St Saviour's church (left). The road had been laid out by 1891 over the former Rhodes farmlands from which Alexandra Park had been formed, and was built up piecemeal from late Victorian times inwards. St Saviour's originated as a Church of England mission in a corrugated iron building opened in 1900 to serve the growing district. The red brick Decorated Gothic style church was designed by local architect J.S. Alder and built 1904-9 to seat 700 people. It was demolished in 1994 for housing development.

(Picture, Dick Whetstone).

Alexandra Park Road, Wood Green, 1905

Alexandra Palace, Wood Green, c.1914

Farmlands to the west of Wood Green were acquired in 1863 and Alexandra Park was laid out and the first Alexandra Palace was built, opened in 1873. Burnt down within 16 days, the palace was rebuilt and reopened in 1875. This pre-First World War view of the 1875 building is of the east side. In 1935 the BBC was to build a television mast on the tower on the left and from its Alexandra Palace studios begin in November 1936 the world's first high definition public television service. In July 1980 fire gutted much of the interior of the Palace but after restoration it was reopened in 1988. It is an exhibition and a conference centre and also houses an ice rink on the east side of the building, opened in July 1990.

(Picture, Dick Whetstone).

When purchased by a consortium of local authorities in 1901, Alexandra Park consisted of 173 acres, of which 154 acres lay within the Urban District of Wood Green. Included was the race course, opened in June 1868 and operating until September 1970. Many racegoers travelled via Wood Green railway station (now renamed Alexandra Palace) or used other transport services such as hansom cabs, seen here leaving the park by the Priory Road, Hornsey, exit.

(Picture, HHS).

Alexandra Park exit, c.1900

Wood Green Public Library, c.1930

The cupola-topped library on the corner of Station Road and Jolly Butchers Hill (right) was opened in September 1907. The £8,569 cost was met by philanthropist Andrew Carnegie who paid for many libraries to be built at this time. In Station Road (beyond the advertisement for the popular Sunday newspaper *Reynolds's News*), among the line of shops, is the entrance to a cinema, opened as the Palais de Luxe, reconstructed in 1931, renamed the Rex in 1946 and closed in 1964. In the 1970s this whole site was redeveloped. The library was demolished in 1973 and a large office block built. The library reopened in a new building adjacent to the Wood Green shopping centre.

(Picture, Bruce Castle).

This was built on the north side of Lordship Lane in 1865 on a 10 acre site which had been occupied by a large house and then by an earlier Masonic school building. It was intended for sons of poor or deceased Freemasons. In 1898 the school moved to Bushey and the building became the Home and Colonial School Society training college. In the 1930s it was bought by the local gas company. It became the offices of Eastern Gas which named it Woodall House after its chairman. In 1974 it was bought by Haringey Council as part of its central area redevelopment plans and much of the site was used for housing. The building has been converted into a Crown Court, opened in 1989.

(Picture, Bruce Castle).

Royal Masonic School, Wood Green, 1902

Royal Masonic School, Wood Green, c.1895

The design of the classroom with double desks on stepped tiers was the norm in the schools built in the late nineteenth and early twentieth centuries and persisted until after the Second World War. Another example can be seen on page 21.

(Picture, Bruce Castle).

Looking east the 1905 Junior School is on the corner of Ellenborough Road. Traffic lights now control the heavy traffic at the intersection of Boreham Road (extreme right) with Lordship Lane. A grocer's shop, now an estate agent's can just be seen on the corner of Boreham Road. The tram service started a year before the school opened, operating between Wood Green at Jolly Butchers Hill and Tottenham via Bruce Grove. A tram can be seen approaching the spot where the Roundway and Downhills Way were laid out in the 1930s. The school was built on land once owned by Graingers Farm and purchased by the British Land Company in 1880. Graingers Farm survived until 1895 to be commemorated by Grainger Road when house building began.

(Picture, Dick Whetstone).

Lordship Lane, Wood Green, 1908

Spouters' Corner, Wood Green High Road, c.1910

Situated on the corner of Lordship Lane and the High Road, this open space is a remnant of the common land which once bordered the road and is now in the ownership of the council. It was dubbed Spouters' corner because it provided a convenient meeting space for orators on political and religious subjects, on the lines of Hyde Park's Speakers' Corner. Some of the shops to the left were demolished in 1931 to make way for Wood Green tube station, though the right hand end of this terrace remains. On the extreme right of the picture are the premises of Willis's, seed merchants and garden suppliers, who long traded here until required to give up the premises when plans were made in the 1970s to redevelop the central area of Wood Green. The same site in 1864 had been occupied by a smithy. The pub sign is for *The Nags Head* on the opposite side of the High Road. The tramcar is a MET type C/1 bound for Finsbury Park.

(Picture, Bruce Castle).

In this view, looking south from the Lordship Lane junction, Spouters' Corner (see page 33) is on the left. The trees in the centre beyond the tram would have stood in Gladstone Gardens, an area of common land retained as a public open space, and situated opposite Gladstone Road. This garden area was to be built on in the 1930s when the Broadway Parade of shops was erected each side of the entrance to a cinema, the auditorium for which was built on the grounds of The Elms, a surviving estate behind the gardens, The cinema, designed by Gaumont architect W.E. Trent, was opened in 1934 as the Gaumont Palace. It was later renamed the Gaumont, then in 1962 the Odeon. The original large auditorium building built to seat 2,500 people, still stands, and was last used for Top Rank Bingo. In 1990 the building was listed Grade II by the Department of the Environment.

(Picture, HHS)

Spouters' Corner, Wood Green, 1906

Barratt's Factory, Wood Green, c.1928

The manufacturing confectioners Barratt & Co., founded in 1848, moved from Islington to a former piano factory in Mayes Road, Wood Green in 1880. They expanded to become an important employer of local labour. The odour of sweets being made, including Barratt's liquorice all-sorts and Caxton chocolate, became familiar in the area. This view of the factory is from across Wood Green Common to the corner of Mayes and Western Roads. Alexandra Board School, built 1897, is on the right. Production finally ceased at Barratt's in about 1980, after about 100 years on the site, and a Social Security office block of c.1985 stands in place of the two-storey building. The tall and imposing Barratt office block (left) survives in modified form without the firm's name on the side, but still with elegant clock dated 1897. Mayes Road and the adjoining Caxton Road (renamed Parkland Road in the 1970s) were laid out by 1864 and villas with 1860s and 1870s date stones are to be seen, including Brighton Villas, dated 1869, still to be found opposite Barratt's office block.

(Picture, HHS).

Looking north up the High Road with Noel Park Railway Station on the right. The Palace Gates- Seven Sisters line opened 7th October 1878, helping the development of Noel Park Estate with cheap fares for workmen on trains linking with the City, Blackwall and Docklands. It also took the thousands of visitors to Alexandra Palace. By 1961 the service had declined to only six 'up' trains a day. That year was the last service of the Eastern Region of British Rail to be operated by steam. The last passenger train ran on the line on 5th January 1963 with an unusually crowded and decorated train departing Palace Gates at 2.00 pm to North Woolwich. The Shopping City and Haringey Central Library were constructed on railway land, completed in 1980.

(Picture, Bruce Castle).

Railway Bridge, High Road, Wood Green, c.1905

High Road, Wood Green, 1905

Looking north, showing the shopping parade which was to be redeveloped in the 1970s as part of Wood Green Shopping City. The wines and spirits shop stood on the corner of Mayes Road, which before redevelopment of the area, used to join the High Road here at a junction with Alexandra Road. The shopping parade has now been replaced by the Shopping City building, with Boots the Chemists occupying the corner site, and the middle distance dominated by the access bridge across the High Road. The road crossing is controlled by traffic lights.

(Picture, Bruce Castle)

The Co-op and later 'Toys R Us' occupied this corner (left of the High Road and Lymington Avenue from early 1980s until 1995. Developers are now dividing the building into six separate shops. The family-owned shops along the north side of Lymington Avenue, have all gone now, including Aberdour Bros., the coal merchants who owned a horse and cart delivering to nearby streets; Bizley's dining rooms: the oil shop selling paraffin, candles and matches: Crossman's, the grocers; Souster's and The Mirror Laundry. Lymington Avenue leads to Noel Park Estate, built from 1883 onwards by the Artizans', Labourers' and General Dwellings Company and named after its chairman, Ernest Noel, MP. At the end of the row of shops can just be seen a bridge where the Palace Gates railway, opened in 1878, crosses the road.

(Picture, Bruce Castle).

Lymington Avenue, Wood Green, 1910

Cheapside, High Road, Wood Green, c.1914

Looking towards Cheapside, on the east side of Wood Green High Road. The domed turret is on the corner of Lymington Avenue and the view can be contrasted with the 1910 picture on page 38. The trees and buildings on the southern side of Lymington Avenue gave way to this parade, which still exists today and carries the date 1911. It forms part of the Noel Park estate to the rear. In the centre of the parade is the entrance to the Wood Green Empire, distinguished by the taller roof line. This theatre opened in 1912 (see page 40). Cheapside, which is named after the Old English word for market, is separately numbered. Edmonds Brothers (centre) was one of two large High Road department stores, the other being Bartons to the south. Electric tramcars were the mode of transport when this view was taken.

(Picture, C. R. Smith Publications).

Opened 9th September 1912 on the east side of Wood Green High Road, the 2,850 seater auditorium was located to the left of the frontage, abutting Lymington Avenue. Films were shown briefly when talkies came in during 1929-30 but mostly the Empire staged live acts and musical shows until it closed on 31st January 1955. In the 1960s it was used for a time by Associated Television mostly for television 'spectaculars'. In the 1970s the auditorium was demolished and the building redeveloped as a Sainsbury's supermarket, with the entrance in Lymington Avenue. The High Road frontage has been converted into shops, with Halifax Building Society occupying the entrance area in 1991. The whole parade is called Cheapside (see page 39).

(Picture, C. R. Smith Publications).

Wood Green Empire, c.1920

High Road, Wood Green, c.1905

This view looks north from a point near Courcy Road and shows the two shopping parades either side of Dovecote Avenue, built for the Artizans', Labourers' and General Dwellings Company. The style is plainer than that of the later Cheapside, whose future site is marked by the trees in the middle distance beyond the second parade (see page 39). Built up towards the end of the nineteenth century and the beginning of the twentieth, Wood Green High Road developed into one of the most important shopping centres in north London. Many of the Victorian and Edwardian parades can still be identified, like the ones in the picture which survive virtually intact, though modern shop fronts have transformed the appearance at pavement level. In the 1970s some parades (like the one on page 37) disappeared when Wood Green Shopping City was built, partly on disused railway land made available by the closure of Palace Gates railway. One feature of the High Road is its width, deriving from its original form, shown on the 1873 Ordnance Survey map as lined with roadside common land and running through fields.

(Picture, Dick Whetstone).

Looking north; Barton's the drapers (right) occupied nos. 26-36 High Road, Wood Green, on the east side. This department store became one of the most prominent and successful in the road. Service was at long wooden counters, with a chair for customers to sit and wait, and the assistant dealing with payments by sending bill and money in a metal container by wires to a central cash-desk.

(Picture Dick Whetstone)

Barton's, High Road, Wood Green, c.1925

Barton's, High Road, Wood Green, c.1960

The same location as page 42 but taken after the Second World War, showing how the store had been modernised. Unfortunately the store was hit by fire in the 1960s and destroyed and was not rebuilt. Other shops now occupy the site, such as British Home Stores.

(Picture, HHS).

The name Westbury may have been taken from Berry Lane the original name of Lordship Lane into which Westbury Avenue runs at the far end. Note the spelling of the name above the door of the Public House. It was a very muddy rutted track back in 1870. The bend just before Boreham Road was made in order to circumvent the south-east tip of the Ducketts estate and pass the main gate to Graingers farm which was not demolished until 1895. A doctor's surgery now occupies the approximate site of the farm house. The British Land Company purchased the farm lands in 1890 to sell to speculative builders who between 1890-1901 built the houses along Westbury Avenue. The odd triangle shaped piece of land at the end of the Terrace between Westbury Avenue and Willingdon Road was not suitable for building but St Marks Church, Noel Park acquired the land and built a corrugated iron hall which was used for mission services. The hall fell into disuse and in 1902 the Baptist Church were able to purchase the "Iron Church" and the plot of land for £900. It was not till 1929 that the Church we see today was finally built. The public house and, on the right hand side, the hardware shop and newsagent are still trading. Behind the camera a bridge carries the Avenue over the site of the railway that ran from Seven Sisters to Palace Gates Station 1878-1963.

(Picture, D.H. Watts & Sons).

Westbury Avenue, Wood Green, c.1907

Green Lanes, Wood Green, 1928

Newent Villas and Pleasant Villas built in 1850 in a classical style on the east side of Green Lanes opposite Ducketts Common. In 1930 the Villas were demolished to make way for the London Transport Bus Station, Turnpike Lane Underground Station, a cinema, restaurant and shops. Westbury Avenue can just be seen on the far left. We know from the census that in 1881, Augusta Field with two daughters, servant and a boarder lived at Newent Villas. The family deriving an income from property they owned. Their neighbour George Forman at Pleasant Villas was a pork butcher, with a wife, his sister, daughter and a servant. The last occupants (in 1927) were Charles Leaver and family who hired out motor cars. Their neighbour at Pleasant Villas was a Miss G. Bennett.

(Picture, Bruce Castle).

Hoardings at the junction with Westbury Avenue conceal the demolition of Newent and Pleasant Villas in preparation for the construction of Turnpike Lane Underground Station and access for tunnel boring. Note the Model T Ford truck coming out of Westbury Avenue and the familiar brand names advertised on the hoardings.

(Picture, Bruce Castle).

Green Lanes, Wood Green, 1930

Green Lanes, Wood Green, 1932

Construction of Turnpike Lane Underground Station on the corner of Westbury Avenue. Four and a half miles of twin tunnel had to be bored, plus three and a half miles of surface work for the Piccadilly Line extension from Finsbury Park to Cockfosters. Fifteen feet of tunnel a day were constructed at a depth of fifty feet at Turnpike Lane Station. 20,000 workers were employed over two and a half years on both the tunnel and surface contracts at a cost of over five million pounds. Charles Holden designed all the stations on the extension, which were built by Prestige and Company. Charles Brand and Son were the tunnel contractors and Sir Robert McAlpine and Sons were responsible for the surface work.

(Picture, London Transport Museum).

This photograph of 9 to 14 Havergal Villas was taken from junction of West Green Road and Green Lanes. The man is standing outside number 14. In 1927 number 9 was the dental surgery of Bernard Du Boisson and at number 10 Miss E.R. Hanson offered Pianoforte lessons. To-day both 9 and 10 are a surgery. Numbers 12, 13 and 14 were demolished in the 1930s for an electricity sub-station. The houses faced (left) Ducketts Common, a public open space, all that remains to-day of the 138 acre Ducketts farm. The farm house survived in Wood Green High Road near Lymington Avenue until 1880 when the rest of the farm land was sold in 1883 to become Noel Park Estate. Tottenham UDC improved Ducketts Common in 1900 laying paths, planting 140 trees and again in 1912 planting a further 30 trees and later laying out hard tennis courts. Haringey Borough Council in 1989 built the children's playground.

(Picture, Bruce Castle).

Green Lanes, Wood Green, 1905

Tottenham

In Roman times, Tottenham High Road was built as part of what we now call Ermine Street, with a low summit at High Cross, itself a possible Roman marker. The eastern parish boundary was the River Lea, an important artery of communication in Roman and Viking times. The Lea gained economic importance in the eighteenth century when the canals were cut, and in the nineteenth century when the London Docks were developed, but this scarcely affected Tottenham whose riverside remained open pasture.

Tottenham's appearance in Domesday Book (1086) implies it existed in pre-Norman times, at least as a farming community. It was entirely rural and sparsely populated with its main settlement at High Cross. Other early settlements were at the Hale and around a number of greens, Duckett's (1293). Page Green (1319), West Green (1384), Beans Green (1393), Chapman's Green (1391), and Wood Green. these were probably farmsteads with associated buildings and labourers' cottages. Wood Green did not become a separate local authority until 1888.

By the sixteenth century a number of rich Londoners had large country retreats built in Tottenham. In addition to Bruce Castle, which already existed, there were the Black House (renamed Ridley) in High Road opposite White Hart Lane. Awlfield Farm next to the church, the moated manor house of Mockings, Ducketts, Asplins, Willoughbies, Crokes, The Priory and five others with more than ten hearths in 1664. Even in the eighteenth century there were few buildings elsewhere — an inn at Tottenham Hale, a mill on the Lea, and a few buildings in Marsh and Willoughby Lanes. West Green had fewer than six houses. Wood Green's houses were widely scattered — Nightingale Hall at Bounds Green and Tottenham Wood Farm near Muswell Hill.

With improved road communication in the nineteenth century, there was a great increase in the building of large villas and houses for professional men in the City. The development of Bruce Grove had taken place in 1789, and as private dwellings increased so there grew a demand for private schools and services from tradesmen, but virtually no industrial development.

The population doubled between 1811 and 1851. In 1840 the Northern and Eastern Railway opened their line along the Lea Valley, but it was not in the populated area of the time and brought development mainly in Tottenham Hale and near Asplins Farm and eastwards from the High Road. New churches and chapels were opened but the population was still only nine thousand. In the 1850s the population increased by four thousand, and in the 1860s by ten thousand causing problems with water supply and sewerage. More rapid growth was taking place in Wood Green where the Great Northern Railway Line had opened in 1850, with a station in 1859.

The most rapid growth in Tottenham came with the arrival of the Great Eastern Railway in 1872 and most Tottenham buildings date from this period and later. The opening of stations on the Tottenham and Hampstead Junction Line at South Tottenham and on the Great Eastern Line through West Green in 1878 hastened the spread of building. The population of Tottenham doubled during the 1870s and reached nearly 100,000 by 1891 so that much of the area was built up then with the pattern of roads and terraces surviving to-day. Certainly many of the shops and houses featured in this publication existed in the first two decades of the century and are still recognisable. In addition, many schools, places of worship, libraries, public buildings and workplaces were being built during this period to service the expanding population.

Tottenham High Road was first laid by the Romans and was known as Ermine Street. When the City of London's walls were built, Bishopsgate provided an exit for the road. It follows higher ground clear of the River Lea, to the northern boundary of Tottenham at Snell's Park, at which point to-day's road bears right, away from the course of the Roman road which gave a direct link to the Roman military centres at Lincoln and York. In later centuries it became the main route from London to Cambridge. On its passage through Tottenham, the road crosses some shallow valleys including the Moselle, causing problems when it was not well maintained in the middle ages. When coach travel needed good surfaces and turnpikes were introduced in 1713, the High Road was described as the worst road near London.

This important line of communication provided custom for inns; some were known to exist in the fifteenth century. Coaches started from the Swan and other inns by 1833, and horse buses were running to the City and West End by 1839. The tramway was started in 1881 and electrified in 1905. Trolleybuses followed in 1938. Motor-bus routes were introduced between 1911 and 1914. The opening of the Northern & Eastern Railway in 1840 did not help the residents of the High Road much since it was expensive, and at a considerable distance to the north of Ferry Lane. In 1872, a better service was provided by the opening of the Great Eastern's Line from Bethnal Green (later Liverpool Street) to Edmonton, with stations at Seven Sisters, Bruce Grove and White Hart Lane. There had always been some ribbon development along the High Road north of Tottenham Green and by 1860 it was lined by buildings backed by open country. Many large properties with extensive grounds were replaced in the early years of the twentieth century by smaller shops and houses which form the basic appearance of the High Road to-day.

Malcolm A. Stokes

Broadwater Farm House, Tottenham, 1892

Showing Andrews's Dairies' milk chariots and handcarts. The farm lay on the south side of Lordship Lane and was occupied at this time by Mr Andrews. In 1926 the land was acquired by Tottenham Urban District Council and opened in 1932 as Lordship Recreation Ground, nearly 100 acres in extent. Moira Close had been laid out on the site of the farmhouse. In the early 1970s part of the site was used to build the Broadwater Farm housing estate.

(Picture, Bruce Castle).

In this view, looking west towards Wood Green, the Broadwater Farm buildings are on the far left. The Moselle river crosses under the white bridge. Some 179 acres of fields on the north side of Lordship Lane (right) were acquired by London County Council at the beginning of the twentieth century and by 1910 some 48 acres had been laid out as the Tower Gardens estate, on 'garden suburb' principles; it is now a conservation area. Adjacent land to the east was used in 1907 by the Peabody Fund to build 154 terraced cottages, still there today.

(Picture, Bruce Castle).

Lordship Lane, Tottenham, 1893

Shell Bandstand Lordship Lane Recreation Ground, Tottenham, 1949

Many forms of entertainment have been staged at the Shell Theatre on fine summer days from ballroom dancing to live shows. The open-air theatre and children's boating pool were opened by the Mayor of Tottenham on 13th June 1936. The theatre has recently been refurbished for live shows to be staged again.

(Picture, Bruce Castle).

Viewed from Lordship Lane. A favourite camping ground for gypsies. One of their caravans stands at the projected Wimborne Road. The cutting for Mount Pleasant Road disappears over the hill. On the opposite side of Lordship Lane is the Peabody Estate, which was to be built in 1907 it consisted of 154 terraced cottages funded by George Peabody. This well known philanthropist was born in America in 1795; became a millionaire and in 1837 settled in London. He gave away several million pounds to charitable causes, mainly to house the poor. In 1862 he gave £500,000 to the City of London as a fund from which the interest was to build housing for the needy. Part of this money was used to construct the Peabody Estate at Lordship Lane. Peabody died in this country in 1869.

(Picture, Bruce Castle).

Mount Pleasant Fields, Tottenham, 1892

Mount Pleasant Fields, Tottenham, 1902

Celebration festivities for the coronation, of Edward VII. The coronation was postponed owing to the King's illness but the children's tea for 10,000 and bonfire took place as planned on June 26th. The bonfire was 36 feet high!

(Picture, Bruce Castle).

Preparing to lay tramlines for the new Metropolitan Electric Tramways Co's route from Wood Green to Bruce Grove, opened in 1904. Looking east, the turning on the right beyond the shops is Mount Pleasant Road, in the distance the Elmhurst Public House and Bruce Castle (left) behind the trees. The fields on the left were to be used in 1907 for the Peabody Estate.

(Picture, Bruce Castle).

Lordship Lane, Tottenham, 1903

Bruce Castle, Tottenham, 1890

Bruce Castle in Lordship Lane is basically a Tudor building, but very much altered in later centuries. It originated as the manor house for Tottenham and its name refers to Scottish royalty who were for a period lords of Tottenham manor. Situated near the mediaeval parish church of All Hallows, Tottenham, it has no record as a castle. In the nineteenth century the building was used as a private school run by the family of which Rowland Hill, the deviser of penny postage in 1840, was a member. When the school was closed Tottenham Urban District Council acquired the estate, in 1891, and opened the 20 acres of grounds as a park. The building was used as a library and museum, the latter established there permanently since 1927. It now houses Harringey's local history archives as well as the borough museum.

(Picture, Bruce Castle).

Numbers 1-16 today form Tottenham's largest concentration of listed buildings. They were built between 1785-1820 and became fashionable houses of the rich, with many Quakers as residents. Along with Northumberland Park and Landsdowne Road, Bruce Grove was considered a very desirable area. Out of view on the right behind the low wall are the Draper's Almshouses built in 1869 on three sides of a quadrangle two stories high, with a Chapel in the centre. Still in use today they were modernised by Haringey council in 1977-9.

(Picture, Bruce Castle).

Bruce Grove, Tottenham, 1893

Bruce Grove, Tottenham, 1904

Celebrating the opening of the Wood Green to Tottenham tram route in 1904. A festooned tramcar of the Metropolitan Electric Tramways stands at the Drapers Almshouses in Bruce Grove. The line ran from Jolly Butchers Hill, Wood Green along Lordship Lane to Bruce Grove. The top-hatted dignitaries appear proud of their achievement. No doubt some were councillors of the Urban District Council and directors of the Metropolitan Electric Tramways board.

(Picture, Bruce Castle).

Looking north west towards Bruce Castle. Bruce Grove Cinema (right) was planned with a dance hall by the Tottenham Cinema and Entertainments Co. in 1920. The company was formed by local people, many working class, who saw the need for both dance floor and cinema. Opened in July 1921, the cinema was reconstructed in 1933 and was still very much in business in 1964, but in 1974 as entertainment tastes changed a new cinema complex was opened in the former dance hall called studios 5, 6, 7 and 8 operating until closing in 1981 when it became a bingo and social club. Today the International Christian Worship Centre and Snooker and Social Club flourish in the building.

(Picture, Bruce Castle).

Bruce Grove, Tottenham, 1928

Bruce House, High Road, Tottenham, 1870

Facing the High Road at the south corner of Bruce Grove, the house was soon to be demolished to make way in 1872 for the Great Eastern railway station. During the 1860s it had become a school with Catherine Keating as headmistress.

(Picture, Bruce Castle).

Bruce Grove railway station, built on the site of Bruce House, opened in 1872. The fare to Liverpool Street Station was 2d. A worker's weekly season ticket cost one shilling on early morning trains. Wilsons builders merchants is on the far left corner of Bruce Grove. Bruce Grove buildings and Maitland Terrace are beyond. The George and Vulture Inn sign can just be seen on the right. Modern shops including a bakers and confectioners, MacDonalds fast food restaurant and a branch of Supersnaps now occupy the site of this ancient Tottenham High Road hostelry.

(Picture, Bruce Castle).

High Road, Tottenham, 1891

High Road, Tottenham, 1893

Bruce Grove Buildings, tenants include G.L. Wilson, builders suppliers; Art Lead Glass works; Lea & Co. Coal Merchants. Lea & Co. had a number of shops in the area taking orders for coal and wood as cooking and most room heating were still by open fires and ranges. Maitland Terrace follows on at number 513. with mens outfitters from 529-535 the High Road. Note the horse-drawn tram picking up passengers.

(Picture, Bruce Castle).

Here Tottenham High Road, looking north, becomes Fore Street, Edmonton. The main road leaves the course of Roman Ermine Street at this point and bears right as indicated by the line of traffic. The old boundary between the parishes of Tottenham and Edmonton is still marked by a line of granite blocks across the road and a clear line across the pavement. Now it is the boundary between the London Boroughs of Haringey and Enfield. The Snell's Park Congregational Chapel on the left was built in 1850 and demolished a century later and a large tower block of flats extends across this view to-day. Fore Street was widened to accommodate trams in 1906. The sign of the *Waggon & Horses,* now the *Coach & Horses* is visible on the right.

(Picture Bruce Castle)

High Road, Tottenham c.1909. The Edmonton Boundary

High Road, Tottenham, 1893. The former Blue Lion Coffee House.

The gabled building was formerly an inn and bears the date 1500 A.D. Two of its timbers may still be seen on an open space where the boundary crosses the road and pavement where Tottenham High Road becomes Fore Street Edmonton. The importance attached to the boundary when this picture was taken is shown by the Tottenham Parish sign by the upper window and the name of 'Boundary House' (partly obscured by 'Selling Off' bills). The old Blue Lion was destroyed by fire in 1894. These buildings were situated a little to the north of the *Waggon & Horses* and around the curve of the road shown in the postcard on page 64

(Picture Bruce Castle)

West side looking south towards Brunswick Court. This stretch of the High Road lies between the Edmonton Boundary and White Hart Lane, just off this picture on the left. The nearest shop on the right was no. 837, Harry Foreman, grocer. Next at 835 was Robert Randall gas fitter, and at 833 Frederick James, oilman. Then at 831, George Goodwin's potato warehouse was by the gap in the shops called Brunswick Court, now Brunswick Square. Continuing on the south side of the opening was Charles Phillips, beer retailer, then James Conn, general smith. Finally came Crusha & Son, printers, who provided offices for the *Tottenham & Edmonton Weekly Herald,* which having been founded in 1861, was acquired by its manager, Edwin Crusha, in 1864. The land behind this facade was occupied by Brunswick Nurseries.

(Picture Bruce Castle)

High Road, Tottenham early 1880s.

High Road, Tottenham, 1910

Looking north with Park Lane junction on the right. The trees formerly in the front gardens of grand villas now shade the Tottenham Sports Centre. The fire station lamp in the right foreground indicates a time when small stations with escape ladders were spread round the locality. The wooden public conveniences on the pavement have since been replaced with a brick structure set further back, threatened in 1991 by Council spending cuts.

(Picture Bruce Castle)

The wall on the extreme right conceals part of the home of George Gripper J.P., now occupied by the premises of a ladies' dress shop. Barrels and a hand cart may be seen belonging to Robert William Chapman, wine and spirit merchant. The shop with a blind is number 682 belonging to Jabez E. Eastman, chemist, which also served as a post office. Partly concealed beyond is the home of Mrs. Abrahams, The Chestnuts, now the site of a large building housing Haringey Rent Offices, and various commercial premises.

(Picture Bruce Castle)

High Road, Tottenham, south of Argyle Passage, early 1880s.

High Road, Tottenham, 1910

The Gas Board, Lordship Lane on the left. In his account, *Tottenham Shops,* H.G. Hawkes writes: 'The green copper domes and the two faces of a large clock beneath an elegant and unique corner still add dignity to the High Road. Its plush interior, warm from so many gas lamps, fires and ovens being demonstrated, was so pleasant when business was completed'. This has since become Haringey's Environmental Centre. On the right of the picture, at the corner of Lansdowne Road, the London Co-op were to build their 1930 store with a large corner tower. This still bears the date and the initials *LCS* and is now Carpetland.

(Picture Dick Whetstone)

Established by public subscription on the the east side of the High Road at Scotland Green, with the school children known by their distinctive school uniform. In 1833 the original building was demolished and replaced with this one, enlarged in 1876. The school was known for a time from 1886 as Tottenham Middle Class School. It was finally closed in 1930 and the buildings converted to shops.

(Picture, Bruce Castle).

The Blue Coat School, High Road, Tottenham 1892

High Road, Tottenham, Burgess's store, 1931

This store will be better remembered as the Co-op, replaced in the 1980's with a supermarket and six small shops. Built in 1923 and called Sanchez House, it was used by Burgess for the sale of household goods and drapery before being taken over by the Co-op. In 1599 the site was owned by Balthazar Sanchez and within twenty years almshouses bearing his name were built in a row of eight single room tenements, brick built, each with its own garden. From the eighteenth century, they were the oldest such buildings in Tottenham and were described as damp and inconvenient in 1825. Their sale was sanctioned in 1919 and they were demolished.

(Picture, Bruce Castle).

West side just north of Bruce Grove. The first shop on the left, partially obscured, was no. 519, that of Mrs. Henrietta Sterlini, confectioner. The Wesleyan and General Assurance Society occupied the upper part of the next two shops which at ground level were Yates & Sons, dyers and cleaners, and Hinton & Co., photographers. A horse tram obscures the next shops but not the sign on the roof of nos. 527 and 529. W. Saville & Co. which was a large shop with pianos and other musical instruments and sheet music.

(Picture Bruce Castle).

High Road, Tottenham, 1900

High Road, Tottenham, 1905. A. Woodward, butcher and provision merchant.

The four adjacent shops of Alfred Woodward were on the eastern side of the High Road. The George & Vulture is out of the picture on the right. The premises occupied, from the right, numbers 492, 494, 496, and 498 High Road in 1905. By 1909 they were occupied by other individual shopkeepers. A. Woodward had another shop in the High Road on the corner of Wembury Road. He is reputed to have brought the first refrigerated mutton to Tottenham.

(Picture, Bruce Castle)

Looking north just south of Bruce Grove junction. There were problems of loading and unloading merchandise for shops even a century ago, and a great many barrels had to be delivered to the many public houses. The sign of the George & Vulture is in the centre, the site now occupied by the Plough public house. There were nineteen public houses in Tottenham and eight in Wood Green in 1890. The premises of Knight Brothers, pawnbrokers, are obscured by the brewer's dray on the right, but their sign is visible.

(Picture, Bruce Castle).

High Road, Tottenham, 1900

High Road, Tottenham, 1908.

Northwards to Forster Road and the Wesleyan steeple. Henry Wesley Bunton (shop left) was an oilman. The tall buildings are King's House Parade with C.J. Russell, corset manufacturer, at no. 455, then Evans and Hayward, fruiterer, and Mrs. Alice Platt, confectioner, who also offered access to a public telephone. Then came C. Nield, photographer, and T. Aldridge, farrier, next to Forster Road, The steeple of the Wesleyan chapel is now replaced by the square block with the cross of St. Mark's Methodist Church.

(Picture, Bruce Castle)

The Tottenham Palace was built in 1908 (see the date stone on the side wall). As a theatre it could accommodate 1500. It has not achieved 'listed' status despite the pleas of the Theatre Trust. It was used first as a music hall then as a cinema, and is now a social club and bingo hall.

(Picture, Dick Whetstone).

High Road, Tottenham, Palace of Varieties.

High Road, Tottenham, Skating Rink and Palace.

The Canadian Royal Skating Rink was built in 1909, just after the Palace (see page 76) It was converted to show films from 1924 to 1926 when it was known as the Canadian Cinema. It is now a dance hall and social club.

(Picture, Dick Whetstone)

The long history of the cross is a mixture of fact and legend. This area was known as Tottenham High Cross in the middle ages. This is not an 'Eleanor' Cross and may have existed even before the time of Queen Eleanor. It is situated on a rise in the High Road. It was formerly made of wood, and in 1580 had four spurs to support it The top was covered with lead. It had sundials on its west and south sides. In 1809 the cross was repaired and covered with cement. As it does not seem to have served as either a market or religious cross, it has been suggested that the original was a survey mark on Roman Ermine Street.

(Picture, Bruce Castle)

High Road, Tottenham and Cross

High Road, Tottenham and Cross, 1905.

This view southwards shows the same location as pages 78 and 80 and gives the nearest view of the skeleton horse on the building in the right. Fred Fisk's *History of Tottenham* tells the story of the horse on the premises of Mr. Colman jnr. the undertaker (see sign below horse). A family called Turner lived next to the grammer school. One son was a farrier, the other a veterinary surgeon. A horse slipped when dragging its load just here and broke a front leg. The vet put it right and was given the horse on the understanding that he was to keep it, so he used it on his rounds. When it died, the vet boiled the carcase and fixed it with iron supports over the premises as a shop sign.

(Picture, Bruce Castle)

A view northwards from opposite the junction with Philip Lane. The Rose and Crown with its magnificent gas lamps is on the right and the Swan on the left. The overhead cables of the newly electrified trams are just discernible. The scene is drab and bare as the shops are about to open in the early morning, and the great amount of advertising is more noticeable. The buildings include Knight Brothers, pawnbrokers; High Cross cottages; Coleman, the undertakers with the skeleton horse on the roof; and the bay windows of the library, converted into five flats in 1994, still recognisable to-day. (Compare pages 78 and 79).

(Picture, Bruce Castle)

High Road, Tottenham, 1905

High Road, Tottenham, 1881.

Eastern side south of High Cross. The shop on the extreme right is John Shepherd's furnishing warehouse and undertaker's, a reminder of times when the local carpenter also made coffins. The premises to-day are still in the hands of funeral directors. Next after the passageway, was John Pate, the butcher at 324; then Joseph Goddard, corn dealer; and Mrs. Agnes Nixon, newsagent. Then came Sutton & Leigh, provision merchants; Tanner & Co., pharmaceutical chemists; William J. Lee, baker; the Rose & Crown, and the High Cross. A knife-board tram approaches with the passengers sitting back to back.

(Picture, Bruce Castle)

The Swan, just north of Philip Lane. The Swan existed by 1455, but has been rebuilt more than once. Note the fire station on the left in a wooden hut for the firemen only. In 1892, the local Board converted the volunteer fire brigade into a paid one and the headquarters was transferred from Coombes Croft to Tottenham Green. The improvement and the escape ladder may be seen outside in the picture of Holy Trinity Church, on page 83. The passing horse trams demonstrate the need for wide roads to allow trams to pass in the centre clear of pedestrians and other traffic on the outside. Many roads had to be widened when they were introduced. A single tram line with passing places from Stamford Hill to Edmonton had been opened in 1881, by the North London Tramways Company. The double lines were laid in 1892, and electric trams with overhead cables started in 1904-5.

(Picture, Bruce Castle)

High Road, Tottenham, July 1892.

High Road, Tottenham, c.1905

Holy Trinity Church and pump at Tottenham Green. The well at the corner of Philip Lane and the High Road was dug in the eighteenth century. In 1859, the local Board of Health altered it, providing a drinking fountain and a conical roof, but by 1883 the water was declared unfit to drink. Holy Trinity Church was consecrated in 1830 and is built of grey brick. To the right is the Green School of 1847, so called because the children wore green uniforms. The fire station was originally an even smaller hut erected on Tottenham Green in 1892, when the headquarters were first at Scotland Green and then at Coombes Croft. (Compare page 82).

(Picture, Bruce Castle)

A hospital was established on Tottenham Green in 1868 when Avenue House on the south east corner was converted into a training establishment by the Evangelical Protestant Deaconeses. A new block was added and alterations and extensions subsequently made. In 1899 the buildings were surrended and became Tottenham hospital. In 1907 its name was changed to Prince of Wales General Hospital. Adjoining property was bought and additional buildings put up, but mid-nineteenth century buildings still flanked the main block. Despite fierce opposition the hospital closed in the late 1980s and in 1993 the building was converted into 38 flats, renamed Deaconess Court. A stone celebrating the opening by Sir George Young Bt. MP of the Tottenham Green Square Development dated 21 May 1993 is to be seen next to two earlier stones, left of the porch.

(Picture, HHS)

Prince of Wales Hospital, Tottenham, 1930

Cottages at Tottenham Hale, 1901.

At the junction with Broad Lane and Ferry Lane, these dilapidated cottages were soon to be condemned, all that remains now is a widened road system. Note the newspaper billboards on the railings, the headlines read: "F.A. Cup Final, Best Story", referring to the Tottenham Hotspur versus Sheffield United match in the F.A. Cup Final at Crystal Palace on 20th April 1901 when 110,820 people attended, a record for any football game in the world at that time. It is said that Tottenham was deserted that afternoon! The score at half time was 1 all and the final score 2 all. The replay was arranged for the following week at Burnden Park, Bolton. Not many Tottenham supporters could afford to travel to Bolton as the Railway Company would not offer reduced fares. But the final score of Spurs-3, United-1, must have pleased them! The Cup was in the South for the first time since 1882.

(Picture, Bruce Castle).

This part of the High Road, looking north, is joined from the left by Seven Sisters Road and West Green Road. (In the foreground the underground toilets have to-day been replaced by the entrance to the Victoria Line). On the left are the blinds of Ward's large department store. Built in 1909, this was one of the earliest steel-framed buildings in Tottenham, allowing large plate glass windows not normally found so early in the century. This spacious and magnificent shop sold high quality goods with money going to the cashier on an overhead system of pneumatic tubes. After lying vacant for a time, the building is now Seven Sisters Market, with multiple lettings.

(Picture, Dick Whetstone).

High Road, Tottenham, The Broadway, after 1909.

Seven Sisters' Trees, Pages Green, Tottenham, 1904.

Seven Sisters takes its name from a circle of seven elm trees, enclosing an ancient walnut tree, which stood at the southern end of Tottenham High Road. In 1840 they were said to be about 500 years old. The tradition is that they were planted by seven sisters who were about to separate. By 1870 the trees had decayed and had been replaced by seven young trees planted a little further to the east. Local resident Mrs. Couchman said in her 1909 memoirs that they had been planted by the seven daughters of Mr MacRae and that seven other trees were planted a little later nearer the High Road by Mrs. Hibbert's seven daughters. In this view it is not clear which trees Mrs. Couchman referred to. On the 31st December 1955 the seven Basten sisters planted seven lombardy poplars near the junction of Seven Sisters Road and Broad Lane.

(Picture, Bruce Castle).

Seven Sisters Road was driven across what was then open country to reach the southern end of Tottenham High Road by Broad Lane in 1833. Laid out in the era before the coming of the railways, the road was designed to increase access to London. Substantial urban development did not occur in the area until Seven Sisters railway station was opened near the junction in 1872. This station was on the line from Liverpool Street to Edmonton which, with stations at Bruce Grove and White Hart Lane as well, was to help transform Tottenham into a heavily built up London suburb. Seven Sisters tube station opened on the new Victoria line in 1968 near the original railway station.

(Picture, Bruce Castle).

Seven Sisters' Corner, Tottenham, c.1910.

Seven Sisters' Corner, Tottenham, 1903.

Horse trams began to run between Stamford Hill and Edmonton via Seven Sisters' Corner in 1881 on a single track which was doubled in 1892. Electrification occurred in the Edwardian era, with the Metropolitan Electric Tramway company running an electric tramcar service from Finsbury Park to Seven Sisters in 1904, and converting the horse tramcar routes. In 1938 trolley buses took over from electric trams and in 1961 diesel buses succeeded the trolleys. Traffic at this junction has increased enormously in recent decades.

(Picture, Bruce Castle).

WEST GREEN

West Green is recorded as a place name in a 1619 map of Tottenham parish and was located in the south western part between Tottenham High Road and Ducketts Green. A lane, running from Tottenham High Road to Green Lanes was first called Black-Hope Lane but later changed to Black Up Lane as it seems the original name was thought to bring bad luck. In recent years it has been renamed West Green Road. Black Boy Lane and Hangers Lane, later renamed St Ann's Road, are also shown on the 1619 map.

By 1840 the Green had a hand-pump, supplied from a fresh water spring, and 18 houses with 90 inhabitants. By 1884 there were over 400 people with a number of large villas, including Gothic House and West Green House near the Green.

St Ann's Church had been built a mile away to the south east much to the annoyance of the local people, who had wanted the first local Church of England place of worship to be sited on West Green Road serving working class families, rather than the large villas further south. The Church was built with a large donation from Fowler Newsam, a Magistrate of Stamford Hill. The building was completed at a cost of £13,000 within ten months, this despite workers' strikes and the need for deep foundations due to loose ground with wet clay. Architect Talbot Bury designed the nave to seat 625 including 100 free seats. (It was the custom at the time in many Churches to pay for your seat). Dr Tait, Bishop of London, consecrated St Ann's Church on 29th July 1861.

Downhills (later Mount Pleasant House) built prior to 1728, was a fine example of some of the many large residences around Tottenham at this time. A new three storeyed mansion, of brick with a pediment and two low wings had been completed by 1789 when it was occupied by Roland Stephenson, a banker. The house was set in several hundred acres with an ornamental garden on the south side and a grove of trees sweeping half a mile down to the Moselle River.

Broadwater Farm on Lordship Lane was part of Downhills Estate and leased to a Mr Phillips and family.

On the death of Roland Stephenson in 1808, the owner Henry Hoare Townsend offered the house and 81 acres, also Broadwater farm and 119 acres, for sale by auction but they were withdrawn. He then lived in the house with his son until his death in 1826. His son leased the house to Reverend Chauncey Townsend, a poet. In 1884 William Hodson a property speculator (he purchased land in the area for house building including 166 acres of the Harringay House estate) purchased the house living there until 1890. Finally in 1892 a Mrs. Cummings leased the house for her school for young ladies. Hodson eventually sold Downhills to the British Land Company, who sold it to Tottenham Urban District Council in 1902. The mansion was demolished and fields built over but the landscaped grounds remain as a public park and recreation ground. Broadwater Farm housing estate was laid out in the early 1970s on some of the land, taking its name from the old farm.

Mrs. J.H. Riddle, a novelist famous in her time, lived for many years in a large villa near St Ann's church. She was very fond of horses and was often seen riding her horse in the streets of Tottenham. Her husband, a civil engineer, was the first to introduce gas stoves into Tottenham but his invention was not a success, the American model being a better version. In one of her novels "Above Suspicion", written in about 1876 appears this description of West Green in around 1860:

> "Sixteen years ago no more rural village could be found within five miles of the General Post Office than West Green. It was utterly in the country as though situated a hundred miles from London, and by a natural consequence it was country in its ways, habits and manners .....
>
> The various lanes leading to it from Stamford Hill, Tottenham, Hornsey and Southgate, were rural, which they certainly are not now. In those days Philip Lane was not a street, with houses all along one side, as is the case at present. Neither had any building societies invaded the sacred quiet of the road, bordered by wheat fields and meadows, which led off to the Queen's Head, then as pretty a roadside public house as the heart of the traveller need have desired to see — now re-fronted, re-decorated, provided with tea gardens and other modern innovations of a like description".

Railways encouraged growth in the area, with stations at South Tottenham at the foot of Stamford Hill in 1871, Harringay Park (later Harringay Stadium) 1880, and St Ann's 1882. All were on the Tottenham and Hampstead Junction Railway. This line linked with the G.E.R. into the City and Dockland in the south east, and in the west to Stroud Green, Upper Holloway and Highgate Road stations.

In July 1872 a better service was provided with the opening of the Great Eastern line from Liverpool Street to Edmonton, with three new stations at Seven Sisters, Bruce Grove and White Hart Lane. The line offered cheap workmen's weekly season tickets costing one shilling.

Then in 1876 the G.E.R. Company bought property adjoining Seven Sisters station for £10,000 and commenced operations for the construction of a railway line that was to serve West Green residents for 85 years. At first the line was to run from Seven Sisters to Palace Gates, Wood Green. They started making bricks and assembling equipment on the fields acquired, soon after 16 houses were demolished. During June of that year the railway construction started, the Bricklayers Arms were demolished to make way for West Green Station and a large goods yard. The first train departed Seven Sisters Station for Palace Gates on 1st January 1878 at 9.10 am. Trains were to run at 30 minutes intervals.

The line eventually ran to Liverpool Street, Blackwall, Stratford and Woolwich (how useful it would be now with the Docklands development), encouraging new housing. Sadly the line, owned by British Rail in later years, closed on a snowy 5th January 1963. The last train was hauled by a diesel engine bearing a holly wreath with a notice R.I.P. Decorated coaches were packed with well wishers, with standing room only (the latter a common occurrence these days!). It departed Palace Gates at 2.00 pm via West Green for

North Woolwich on its final journey.

By 1900 the West Green area appeared very much as we know it to-day. The North Eastern Fever Hospital on the south side of St Ann's Road opened on 19 acres in 1892. Sanger's Circus used to Winter on a piece of land (with terraced houses now) between Philip Lane and West Green Road. When Sangers set off for their Summer tour, the procession stretched from the Green to Turnpike Lane with hundreds of people lining the road watching the free display.

By 1913 the Imperial Cinema (number 290 West Green Road) was a big attraction with seating for 472 patrons, showing all the latest films. There were always long queues on Saturdays. Renamed the Essoldo in the 1940s and refurbished with an enlarged capacity of 550 seats showing two popular programmes a week, the cinema closed in 1958. It is now a carpet warehouse.

The Fox Public House on the corner of West Green Road and Vincent Road had a fine cricket pitch near the building which happy proximity on a summers day pleased both Landlord and Player. The pub was renamed the Silver Lady in the early 1980s was purchased by the Roman Catholic Church, Diocese of Westminster in 1992 for future development.

Work was to be had at the Mathews Cycle Manufacturers on West Green Road. In 1909 the firm started making Roller Skates for the new craze of roller skating at the many rinks that were opening such as nearby Canadian Royal Skating Rink in Tottenham High Road, now the Ritzy Disco.

Railway work paid a Guinea a week. Clay potteries in White Hart Lane and Williamsons Potteries in Harringay were looking for labour. Factories at Tottenham Hale employed skilled workers in the manufacture of rubber goods. And West Green and Seven Sisters Railway Stations provided a means of transport to work further afield.

West Green is well endowed with open spaces thanks to the foresight of our forebears. Chestnuts House and 13 acres adjacent to Cornwall and St Ann's Road were purchased by Tottenham UDC in 1898 to become Chestnuts Recreation Ground. The House was demolished in the mid 1980s to make way for a fine Borough of Haringey Leisure Centre. The site of Downhill's House, demolished in 1902 by Tottenham UDC, and its 26 acres with a further 4 acres bought from the G.E.R. in 1902, now forms Downhill's Park. The UDC also purchased 54 acres from the Townsend Estate in 1926. With a further gift of 43½ acres, they laid out Lordship Recreation Ground to the north.

West Green to-day is a pleasant place, but not perhaps as peaceful, as in the days of the village pump.

Peter Curtis.

Philip Lane, West Green, 1911

A busy mixed residential and shopping road much as it is to-day. The camera is positioned on the corner of Downhills Park Road. East is St Philip the Apostle's Church on the corner of Clonmel Road, the foundation stone was laid in 1906. On the right is the smart and double-fronted grocers shop of George Munnery. His next door neighbour, Mr John Adams Wigley at number 205, was a corn dealer, no doubt selling fresh bread as the gold lettered "Hovis" sign above the shop suggests. A "Hovis" sign is still there to-day. On the east end of the building on the corner of Summerhill Road a date stone indicates the terrace was built in 1859.

(Picture, Bruce Castle).

The house was approached from Philip Lane up a short drive, along the line of present-day Downhills Park Road. This Victorian photo shows the three-storeyed brick mansion with pediment which by 1789 had replaced an earlier house on this ancient estate. Sold to the British Land Company in 1881, the property passed into the hands of Tottenham Urban District Council. The house was demolished in 1902 and Downhills Park created. The area to the north was to be saved as Lordship Recreation Ground. For a time early in the nineteenth century the house was known as Mount Pleasant (In 1865 another house called Mount Pleasant was built to the east which was sold in 1890 for building; it gives its name to adjacent Mount Pleasant Road).

(Picture, Bruce Castle).

Downhills House, West Green, 1891

The Conservatory Downhills Park, West Green, c.1910

Little remains now of the many ornamental features. A splendid grove of hornbeams, some of which still stand, were considered as some of the best in the country. The park was laid out in 1902-04 in the gardens of Downhills House. The land had been earmarked for house building, but local residents campaigned and, after many public meetings, the park was started.

(Picture, Bruce Castle).

Some of the 330 acres of the Downhills Estate were used to create the park. Hard tennis courts were added in 1936. The Italian Gardens were considered to be an ideal place for a family stroll, maybe to take afternoon tea in the tea house.The park superintendent's lodge can be sen near the water tower should any trouble arise.

(Picture, Bruce Castle).

Italian Gardens, Downhills Park, West Green, 1934

West Green Road, West Green, 1908

Looking west from the Green with Blackboy Lane beyond the shop blind on the left. Horse and cart delivery vehicles wait at the kerb. It was possible in those days to take a train from West Green Station (just off the picture right) to Liverpool Street. West of the Station (closed in 1963) were three coal merchant, William Ray, Potato Merchants, at number 258, and The National Telephone Company Ltd. at number 262; telephone calls could be made from their office. The Black Boy Public House comes next, still a favourite for a pint of well-kept bitter. On the left side at the corner of Clinton Road stands the National Provincial Bank with imposing facade, which had recently moved from less spacious premises further along the road. Next door at Number 263 is Lovit Coltman, Butcher, and at 265 the Florence Dining Rooms, K.K. McCools Public House a cosy free house, now occupies these buildings. On the corner of Black Boy Lane at number 269 is John Craigen one of the numerous beer retailers West Green supported at that time. The Vicarage Parade of shops numbers 1-10 built c.1903 follows, up to the corner of Abbotsford Avenue where at number 293 was the practice of Doctors J. & R. Spears, Physicians and Surgeons. The building still serves the community in a healing capacity, as a Dentist's Surgery. The Colonial Stores Ltd. at number 301 is now a Pet shop.

(Picture, Dick Whetstone).

Looking west from the junction with Tottenham High Road towards the railway bridge constructed in 1872 to carry the G.E.R. line from Edmonton to Liverpool Street. The shops were bustling with customers particularly on Fridays and Saturdays after pay day. The photograph was taken from near Marks and Spencers Penny Bazaar at numbers 9-11 on the corner of Suffield Road. The shop with the magnificent row of gas lamps is number 27, Nolan Denney Provision's Merchants. The shop with the blind on the corner of Westerfield Road is number 29, Edward Albert Coates, Butcher's. Part of the sign advertising Griffiths and Company, Grocers at number 31 can be seen on the opposite corner. The premises are now occupied by an insurance company. At Number 33, Giosue Olgiati's Restaurant catered for the shoppers. Across the road on the corner of Portland Road under the sign "Booksellers and Printers" at number 40 George Warbey, Stationer now Village Bakery. A milk float waits outside number 38 John Hartin, China Dealer, his neighbour at number 36, is Lush and Cook Ltd., Dyers.

(Picture, Dick Whetstone).

West Green Road, West Green, 1908

West Green Road, West Green, 1911

The shops in West Green Road can be compared with those of Ridley Road Dalston and Chapel Street, Islington as favoured shopping venues. The large number of butchers, fishmongers, drapers, greengrocers, wine and beer merchants and stalls drew large crowds each Saturday. After eight in the evening, meat was sold off cheaply as few butchers had cold storage to keep meat fresh over the week-end. At Christmas it might be ten o'clock before the shops closed. Looking west from the corner of Brunswick Road (left) Fredrick Hargroves, Butchers at number 51, perhaps that is Mr Hargroves wearing the straw boater. The premises are now Jafi's Take Away Restaurant. Freeman Hardy and Willis Ltd. trade under their sign, they can still be found in many High Streets. West Green Supermarket occupy the shop to-day. Part of the Railway Tavern (right) is visible on the corner of Beaconsfield Road, later renamed West Green Tavern with the Olympia Stores opposite at number 70.

(Picture, Dick Whetstone).

The original Green Gate Beer House on the corner of Willow Walk and West Green Road built in 1854 by a Mr Hiller as a shop and managed by William Pettit. A beer house licence was obtained in 1862. It soon became the favourite meeting place for locals, like the group posing for the camera. The Green Gate we know to-day was rebuilt by the Stag Brewery in 1931.

(Picture, Bruce Castle).

West Green Road, West Green, 1870

HARRINGAY

Although the line of Green Lanes is of ancient origin, the district known as Harringay, which extends along it from Turnpike Lane south almost to Finsbury Park and the Manor House, dates only from the late nineteenth century. It takes its name from Harringay House, whose wooded and landscaped grounds formerly occupied the whole of the area west of Green Lanes to the Great Northern Railway line. Harringey House itself stood on a knoll about half a mile south-east of Hornsey Station, close to the top of present-day Allison and Hewitt Roads. The last owner of the estate, Edward Chapman, died in 1869, and after a ten-year period during which the property was let it was disposed of by the executors. In the early 1880s the estate was acquired by the British Land Company, which laid out the roads and sold off the land in building plots. No buyer could be found for Harringay House itself, which was demolished about 1885. Wightman Road was constructed to follow the line of the railway on the west of the estate, with nineteen parallel roads running eastwards from it to Green Lanes. The pattern formed by these roads on the map has led to the modern nickname for this area, 'The Ladder'.

The speed of development appears to have made a deep impression on contemporary observers. Writing in the Golden Jubilee edition of the *Hornsey Journal* in 1929, the editor gave his recollections of the period of change in the 1880s:—

> "It was at Harringay that the first great transformation occurred. There was one large house there — derelict I believe — surrounded by forlorn acres across which the adventurous could trespass ... Then came a change. Roads were made and houses built with feverish activity, and I think I am right in saying that within twelve months two thousand persons were living where there had previously been only a deserted and decaying mansion ... Harringay was the scene, I believe, of the first of the big building operations in the district, of the mass production method, under which houses came not as single spies but in battalions ..."

Other developments accompanied or quickly followed the spread of housing. Haringey [*sic*] Passage, left between the buildings to provide a north-south footway across the estate, rather unromantically marked the line of the outfall sewer. Gatherings for religious worship organised the erection of temporary and then permanent buildings to house their congragations. For the Church of England, St Paul Harringay was built at the corner of Burgoyne and Wightman Roads in 1891. This church was destroyed by fire in March 1983, but the distinctive twin spires of St Peter Wightman Road (1898) can still be seen at the corner of Lausanne Road, although the building has been rededicated to St John and is now used for Greek Orthodox worship. The presence of families with children led to the establishment of many private schools, and after some years of controversy Harringay's first Board School was opened in Falkland Road in 1893. Shops opened near Hornsey Station, and also along Green Lanes, where the most ambitious parade, Cavendish

Terrace between Cavendish and Burgoyne Roads, is dated 1892; further north on this side of the road, the facades bear dates later in the 1890s. Public transport was not slow to cater for the new district: Harringay Park Station was opened as early as 1880 at the point where the Tottenham and Hampstead Junction Railway crossed Green Lanes, and in 1885 the Great Northern Railway opened Harringay West by the top of Burgoyne and Umfreville Roads. The horse tram service along Green Lanes from the Manor House to Wood Green was converted to electric traction in 1904.

As the developers moved in on the Harringay House estate, the land on the opposite side of Green Lanes, south of St Ann's Road, was occupied by the farmland belonging to St John's Lodge, which stood on St Ann's Road near the foot of Blackboy Lane. Its field had already been cut through when the Tottenham and Hampstead Junction Railway opened in 1868, and in 1887 the St John's Lodge Farm Estate was sold at auction, to be developed during the closing years of the nineteenth century and early twentieth century. From the outset this area was included, both by street directories and in common usage, under the district of Harringay. The developers of St John's Lodge Farm, faced with an established population on the west side of the main road, felt able to draw up plans for shopping provision on a comprehensive scale: The result was Grand Parade, stretching from St Ann's Road south to the railway bridge, for which the plans were passed in 1899. In the same year the Salisbury Hotel was opened on the corner of St Ann's Road; in its way it may have been even more welcome than shops to residents on the Harringay House estate, since the extreme respectability of the development on the west side of Green Lanes had involved the exclusion of public houses, and there were no premises licensed for drinking between the old-established Queen's Head at Ducketts Common and the small Railway Hotel close by Harringay West Station.

The name of Harringay was brought to a wider audience with the opening in 1927 of the greyhound racing stadium on a site which had originally been a tile works (Bean's Green) and later Williamson's Potteries. It was just south of the Tottenham and Hampstead Junction Railway, next to Harringay Park Station which was later renamed Harringay Stadium. It remained popular until long after World War II, but falling receipts finally led to the closure of the track in 1987, and the station has been renamed Harringay East.

The reorganisation of London's local government in 1965 brought together the previously independent boroughs of Hornsey, Tottenham, and Wood Green (the latter once part of Tottenham parish) into a single administrative unit. Harringay, lying across the boundaries of Hornsey and Tottenham and occupying a central position in the proposed new area, was an early suggestion as a suitable name for the new borough. In the event the authorities opted for the name but in the more archaic spelling 'Haringey' which has caused a certain amount of confusion ever since. Both spellings are in fact forms of the same name from which Hornsey is derived.

Susan Hector

Wightman Road, Harringay, 1908

The picture shows Wightman Road, Harringay's western boundary, looking north from a point opposite Mattison Road. The scene is very little changed today, except for the traffic — it would now rarely be possible to stand in the middle of the road to take a photograph. The Great Northern Railway line runs close behind the houses on the left. On the right, the gable end with chimney-breasting marks the end of Pemberton Road, and further down Wightman Road the tracks left by turning vehicles indicate the location of Warham Road. At the other side of the dip Wightman Road curves to the right, rising slightly; just out of sight it straightens out as it passes the point where Harringay House formerly stood near the top of Alison and Hewitt roads. Twenty-five years earlier this scene would have been one of open parkland, with Harringay House just visible in the distance. Sadly, however, no pictures of the house itself seem to have survived.

(Picture, Dick Whetstone).

The impressive Salisbury Hotel, opened in 1899, had as its first manager R.J. Brinkley, whose name appears on the facade in this view. The builder and architect was John Cathles Hill (1858-1915), an enterprising Scotsman who was also responsible for the Queen's Hotel in Crouch End and a good deal of the local housing development of this period; he also founded the London Brick Company. The Salisbury's size reflects the fact that it was designed to provide all the facilities associated with a residential hotel on the grand scale. In the early 1970s, an observer from the Victorian Society noted a vast disused ballroom upstairs, and met local residents who could still recall uniformed doormen at the entrances. On the Green Lanes side, a lobby gives access to two sets of double doors, the left-hand one leading to the Saloon Bar; the other, now apparently boarded up from the inside, still bears the words *HOTEL ENTRANCE* in peeling gilt letters on the incised glass door panels. The electric tram in the picture puts the date at no earlier than 1904; it is possible that the view was taken to mark the completion of Grand Parade, running south from the Salisbury, about the middle of the decade.

(Picture, HHS).

The Salisbury Hotel and Grand Parade, Harringay, c.1905

Green Lanes, Harringay, c.1930.

This later view is taken from further north than the preceding picture, and shows, in addition to the Salisbury Hotel and Grand Parade, the Coliseum cinema on the left. This opened in about 1912 on the north corner of St Ann's Road, formerly Hanger Lane, the direct route to Stamford Hill. When the extension of the Piccadilly Line from Finsbury Park was announced in 1929, with proposed stations at Manor House and Turnpike Lane, the Harringay Ratepayers' Association led a spirited campaign for an additional station at this junction by the Salisbury. The railway company were politely adamant that the required average speed of trains over the full route would not permit this concession, and the campaigners were eventually obliged to desist.

(Picture, Dick Whetstone).

Looking north past the Salisbury to the Coliseum from a point near Warham Road, and showing on the right the first half-dozen shops in Grand Parade. In this view the main facade of the cinema can be seen, set on the corner of St Ann's Road. Originally named the 'Electric Coliseum', it had a seating capacity of 641, and was popular and well-patronised until well after World War II. It finally closed in June 1961, and after periods as a Bingo club and a warehouse it is now derelict. Just to the north of the Coliseum was built in the 1920s Salisbury Promenade, a two-storey range faced in cream ceramic tiles, with lock-up shops at pavement level (these included, originally, a branch of Woolworths). The upper floor is divided into two large areas, and was originally occupied by a billiard club in the northern section, and the fashionable Salon Bal to the south: this rapidly became a favourite resort for concerts, receptions and dances (its floor was advertised as 'unique'). The Salon Bal was gutted by fire in July 1932, fortunately in the early hours of the morning without causing injury, and the flames were prevented from spreading to a neighbouring timberyard or the houses in Harringay Road behind. The roof timbers of the Coliseum were slightly affected, but it was able to open as usual later in the day. Woolworths subsequently moved south to larger premises at 17 to 19 Grand Parade, but this branch was closed in 1985.

(Picture, Bruce Castle). ***Grand Parade, Green Lanes, Harringay, c.1920***

Grand Parade, Green Lanes, Harringay, c.1910

Looking south from the corner of Chesterfield Gardens, which seems to have been the last of the residential turnings on the St John's Lodge Farm estate to be developed: the 1903 directory records no residents there, although houses in Stanhope Gardens had been occupied since 1898, and in the other turnings by 1902. By the latter date the construction of Grand Parade was well advanced, and Hughes Bros, drapers, are listed as the first occupants of nos. 34, 35 and 36, the three shops south of Chesterfield Gardens. Today nos. 34 and 35 are occupied by the well-known family furniture business of Disney's established in 1913.

(Picture, Dick Whetstone).

This view looking north from a point near the foot of Umfreville Road shows almost the entire length of Grand Parade and illustrates the unity of its design. The one exception is the square building on the south corner of Stanhope Gardens, to which the tall chimneys belong: this was built for the London & Provincial Bank and predates the Parade; in the 1898 directory it was listed (E.B. Ridgway, Manager) in splendid isolation in the stretch of Green Lanes between Harringay Park Station and St Ann's Road. Barclays Bank now occupies the premises. A very visible change in recent years has been to the building on the north corner of Stanhope Gardens, which has lost its top storey with distinctive mansard roof and dormer window, while the other two storeys above the shop are derelict. On the left of the picture, just beyond the tram standard, can be glimpsed the shop premises on the corner of Burgoyne Road. This was a wine and spirit merchant from the early 1890s, and no doubt popular with the residents of the Harringay House estate, being strategically placed for those returning by train to Harringay Park Station.

(Picture, Dick Whetstone).

Grand Parade, Green Lanes, Harringay, 1906

Green Lanes, Harringay, 1905

The Cottages were built for Williamson's Pottery and Brick workers near what is now Williamsons Road. They were condemned by the Medical Officer of Health Dr J.F. Butler in 1905. At the far end of the cottages the west side of Green Lanes near the Beaconsfield Public House can be seen. Williamson's Potteries were one of four in the area. Others were Bounds Green Pottery making tiles (1852-1900), Samuel South (1868-1950) and Coles Potteries (1860-1950), both the latter making flower pots at White Hart Lane. They used local clay, including in the 1930s clay dug from the Piccadilly line tunnel excavations.

(Picture, Bruce Castle).